MORLEY LIBRARY

3 0112 1042 1222 7

W9-AIA-139

THE STORY BEHIND

COAL

Barbara A. Somervill

Heinemann Library
Chicago, Illinois

www.heinemannraintree.com
Visit our website to find out
more information about
Heinemann-Raintree books.

To order:
☎ Phone 888-454-2279
💻 Visit www.heinemannraintree.com
to browse our catalog and order online.

© 2012 Heinemann Library
an imprint of Capstone Global Library, LLC
Chicago, Illinois

Visit our website at www.heinemannraintree.com

All rights reserved. No part of this publication may be
reproduced or transmitted in any form or by any means,
electronic or mechanical, including photocopying,
recording, taping, or any information storage and retrieval
system, without permission in writing from the publisher.

Edited by Megan Cotugno and Diyan Leake
Designed by Philippa Jenkins
Original illustrations © Capstone Global Library Ltd.
Illustrated by Philippa Jenkins
Picture research by Hannah Taylor and Mica Brancic
Production by Eirian Griffiths
Originated by Capstone Global Library
Printed in China by CTPS

15 14 13 12 11
10 9 8 7 6 5 4 3 2 1

Library of Congress Cataloging-in-Publication Data
Somervill, Barbara A.
  The story behind coal / Barbara A. Somervill.
     p. cm.—(True stories)
  Includes bibliographical references and index.
  ISBN 978-1-4329-5434-5 (hb)
  1. Coal. I. Title.
  TN801.S67 2012
  553.2'4—dc22   2010042101

Acknowledgments
The author and publishers are grateful to the following for
permission to reproduce copyright material:
Alamy Images pp. 13 (© World History Archive), 14
(© Lordprice Collection), 15 (© North Wind Picture
Archives), 27 (© Inga Spence); Corbis pp. 9 (Visuals
Unlimited), 16 (Bettmann); Getty Images pp. 19 (Steve
Eason), 22 (Time & Life Pictures/Grey Villet.), 23 (Time
& Life Pictures/Bill Pierce), 25 (Science Faction/Karen
Kasmauski); Library of Congress pp. 17, 18, 20, 21; Mary
Evans Picture Library p. 12 (Rue des Archives/Tallandier);
Shutterstock pp. 4 (© Joshua Haviv), 11 (© lrafael), iii (©
SeDmi), 5 (© Bronskov), 10 (© airphoto.gr).

Cover photograph of coal miner's hand with
coal reproduced with permission of Photolibrary
(Photononstop/J-Charles Gérard).

We would like to thank Ann Fullick for her invaluable help
in the preparation of this book.

Every effort has been made to contact copyright holders of
any material reproduced in this book. Any omissions will
be rectified in subsequent printings if notice is given to the
publisher.

Disclaimer
All the Internet addresses (URLs) given in this book were
valid at the time of going to press. However, due to the
dynamic nature of the Internet, some addresses may have
changed, or sites may have changed or ceased to exist since
publication. While the author and publisher regret any
inconvenience this may cause readers, no responsibility for
any such changes can be accepted by either the author or
the publisher.

Contents

Some words are shown in bold, **like this**. You can find out what they mean by looking in the glossary.

The Rock That Burns

▲ Coal-burning power stations produce the electricity used to light this bridge and buildings.

You may not realize it, but you use coal every day. For example, you turn on a light switch, which uses electricity. Coal **fuels** the power stations that produce this electricity. You ride in cars or on bikes, and coal is used to make the steel in those products. You walk on cement sidewalks, and coal fuels the production of cement. You take an aspirin, add **fertilizer** to a rose bush, or swing a tennis racket. Coal products help to make these items, too.

What is coal?

Coal is a rock found on Earth's surface or deep underground. **Mining** is the process of taking coal from Earth. About 60 percent of coal production worldwide comes from underground **mines**. However, some countries, such as Australia and the United States, get most of their coal from surface mines.

Uses for coal

When coal burns, it produces heat energy. This energy is used to make electrical power and many products.

Even after it is burned, coal gives us useful products. A kind of solid waste product called **coke** is used in producing steel, **pig iron**, zinc, and lead. It is also used to make soda ash, an ingredient found in soap, glass, and paper. **Fly ash** is made up of tiny pieces of burned coal. It is used in making concrete, bricks, and cement. Some fertilizers, which help plants grow, also contain fly ash.

Products made using coal

The following products (and more) are made using coal:

- aspirin
- bricks
- fertilizer
- glass
- mountain bikes
- paper
- steel
- tennis rackets.

▼ **Burning coal creates useful energy.**

How did coal form?

The coal we use today formed starting between about 300 and 100 million years ago. The different materials used to make coal were **deposited** at different times.

Enormous swamps filled with plant life once covered Earth's **tropical** areas, meaning areas with hot, often wet climates. Millions of years ago, northern Russia and midwestern North America were tropical.

When the plants in these areas died, they formed thick layers, called **peat**. Over time, soil and water covered the peat, which did not rot away. The dirt and water were heavy, and this put the dead plants under great **pressure**. Earth's heat combined with that pressure and formed coal. The greatest heat and pressure produced the hardest coal. The least heat and pressure created soft coal, called **lignite** (see page 8).

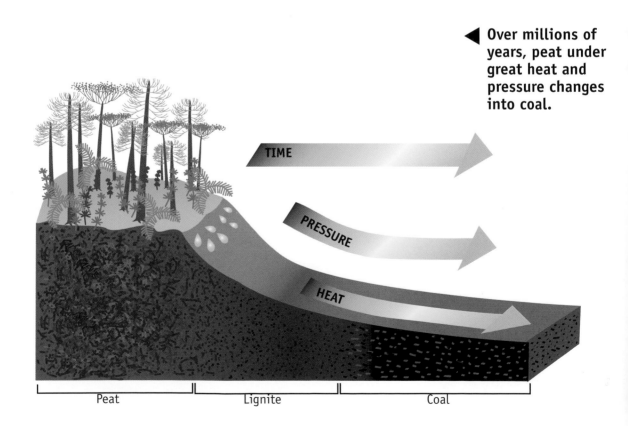

◀ Over millions of years, peat under great heat and pressure changes into coal.

TIME

PRESSURE

HEAT

| Peat | Lignite | Coal |

How much coal is there?

Top-five coal reserve countries	Approximate amount in reserve in millions of tons as of 2006
United States	271,877
Russia	173,074
China	126,215
India	101,903
Australia	86,531

Source: BP Statistical Review of World Energy, June 2007

Over millions of years, Earth slowly shifted, and so areas with coal deposits are no longer tropical. As this map of worldwide coal deposits shows, some of today's tropical areas, such as those in Africa and South America, have no coal at all. These regions did not have large amounts of plant life when coal first began to form.

▼ **Areas with coal deposits were once tropical swamps.**

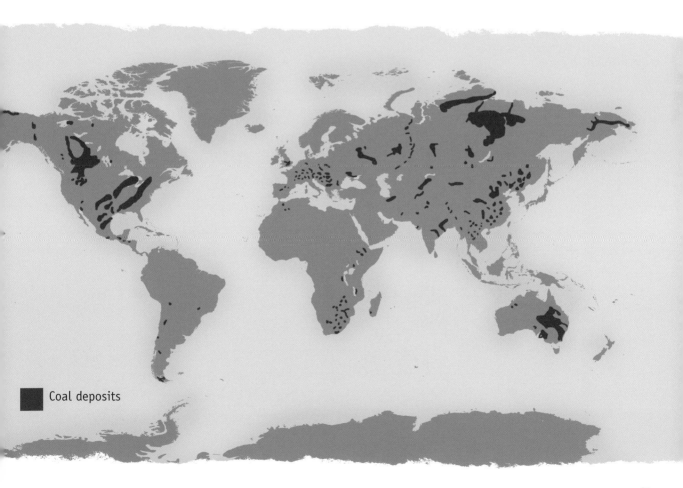

■ Coal deposits

Coal: Fuel and More

Peat

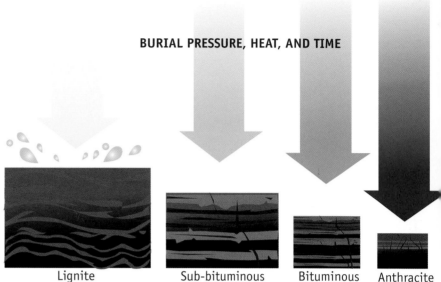

BURIAL PRESSURE, HEAT, AND TIME

Lignite

Sub-bituminous

Bituminous

Anthracite

▲ **More pressure, heat, and time produce harder coal.**

Lignite fly ash ✔

In India, scientists have discovered that lignite fly ash is an effective **insecticide** on vegetable and rice plants. More than 50 different insects avoid chewing on stems and leaves dusted with fly ash.

Coal includes four commonly found varieties: lignite, **subbituminous**, **bituminous**, and **anthracite**. All coal contains carbon, along with hydrogen, oxygen, nitrogen, sulfur, and other substances. These are all **elements**, which are chemical substances that cannot be divided into smaller substances. Coal can be soft or hard, and each type of coal produces different amounts of heat.

Lignite

Miners give lignite lots of different names, such as leonardite, mined lignin, brown coal, or slack. It is a brownish-black coal that contains the lowest amount of carbon of all coals. Nearly 80 percent of lignite coal is burned to generate, or create, electricity.

Burning lignite produces large amounts of fly ash, which is used in concrete, bricks, and cement. Lignite is mined worldwide, including in Australia, Europe, Asia, and North America.

Subbituminous coal

Subbituminous coal is black and holds moisture. It contains about 35 to 45 percent carbon. Subbituminous coal is mostly found in North America and Europe. Sometimes large amounts of subbituminous coal have burst into flame on their own.

How hot does coal burn?

The heating content of coal is measured in British thermal units (BTUs). You need about one kilogram (two pounds) of lignite to produce the same amount of heat as about half a kilogram (one pound) of anthracite.

Type of coal	BTUs per pound
Lignite	4,000—8,000
Subbituminous	8,000—13,000
Bituminous	10,500—15,000
Antracite	About 15,000

▼ **Lignite is a brown, crumbly type of coal.**

9

Bituminous coal

Bituminous coal is an inky-black, medium-hard coal. The United States has large bituminous coal deposits, but China is the world's biggest producer of this coal. Bituminous coal is used to generate electric power and to make steel, pig iron, zinc, and lead. It heats the ovens that fire bricks, tiles, and ceramic pots and vases.

Anthracite

Anthracite is a hard, **metamorphic** rock, meaning it is formed under great amounts of heat and pressure. There is very little anthracite coal in the world. In the United States, anthracite amounts to less than one percent of all coal. Most anthracite is used to generate electricity and for steel manufacturing.

▼ Burning coal at this power plant produces steam. The steam turns machines called **turbines**, which create electricity.

Early coal use

Historians have to guess how people discovered that coal burned. One idea is that thousands of years ago, cave dwellers in Europe found some strange black rocks. They used the rocks to line a fire pit and found that the rocks burned. The rocks gave off heat, which was useful in a cold rock cave.

About 3,000 years ago, Chinese miners dug for coal in the Fu-shun mine in northeastern China. Hot coals **smelted** (melted) copper, which the Chinese used to make coins, bells, and other metal goods. The Chinese also used coal for heat and cooking.

Aztec coal use

The Aztec people, who lived in present-day Mexico City, understood the value of coal. By the 1300s, they used coal for cooking, firing clay pots, and heating. They also used hard coal for jewelry.

◀ **The Aztecs fired pots like this one over hot coals.**

Underground Mining

▲ Bell-pit mines often caved in, making the work dangerous.

Long before the Romans invaded Britain in 43 CE, the Britons used and mined coal in the Forest of Dean. Pieces of coal also fell from cliffs, and coal washed up on beaches. Collecting this coal was easy. But when it ran out, Britons found a way to get more coal. They used axes made from a hard stone called flint to hack coal from Earth's surface. Eventually, the coal available through this method also ran out.

There was more coal below the surface, but how did people get to it? The solution was underground mines.

Early mines

By the 1500s, British religious men called monks had begun **bell-pit** mining. In this method, men were lowered into a fairly shallow pit. The men spent 10 to 12 hours a day digging coal with pickaxes, breathing foul air, and getting little rest. Horses and pulleys or men turning cranks called **winches** raised the mined coal to the surface.

In 1575 Sir George Bruce opened a "moat" pit beneath the Firth of Forth, a large bay in Scotland. Bruce's mine was an early **shaft**-style mine, in which a deep passage was dug into the rock. This was a major advance in mining, but only slightly safer than bell-pit mining.

Digging mine shafts led to the **room-and-pillar** mining technique. Miners cut coal from shaft walls, but left large sections of coal in place to support the ceiling. As mining continued, digging created large rooms and supportive pillars. Pillars were mostly coal and could not be mined. Without the pillars, the mine would have caved in.

▶ **Miners used sledgehammers to break coal into smaller pieces.**

13

Mining superstitions ✓

Miners developed odd fears or superstitions about the dangers of mining. For example, it was believed that if a miner met a pig on the way to work, disaster would follow. That miner returned home rather than bring disaster into the mine.

Inventions improve mining

By the early 1600s, Great Britain had become Europe's major coal producer. Several hundred ships delivered British coal to London and other European cities. But mining coal was not without its costs. Bell-pit and room-and-pillar mines suffered frequent cave-ins. Air quality in mines was poor, and mines flooded. Miners suffered sickness, injuries, and death for the profits that filled mine owners' pockets.

One major problem in coal mines was water seeping into the passages. In 1698 British inventor Thomas Savery created a steam engine that could pump 270 liters (71 gallons) of water a minute. Fourteen years later, Thomas Newcomen and John Calley produced an "atmospheric engine," which ran on air pressure and pumped water faster than Savery's engine.

► The "atmospheric engine" was used for more than 50 years in British coal mines.

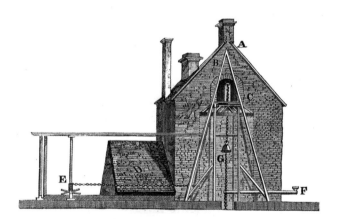

14

The late 1600s brought a better method of mining coal. **Longwall** mining began in Shropshire, England. In this method, workers removed coal from along one wall. The emptied area then caved in behind the miners. This was dangerous! The wall was about 1.8 meters (6 feet) high, and at least 30 meters (100 feet) long. As miners worked, a "pit pony" and a boy came around to collect buckets of coal.

▲ Pit ponies hauled tons of coal daily from coal mines.

15

Coal mining in the colonies

In the 1700s, people in the American colonies began mining coal on a larger scale. In 1748 the first colonial coal mine began operating near Richmond, Virginia. Coal was moved from the mines to manufacturing plants along the James River. Pennsylvania coal mining began at about the same time. Pennsylvania became the one of the largest U.S. coal producers. Its coal fed the furnaces of the growing iron and steel industries.

The Industrial Revolution

The Industrial Revolution was a period beginning in the late 1700s when manufacturing changed from handwork to machine work. Steam engines—many based on a 1774 design by Scottish inventor James Watt—were coal-powered and made factories more productive. As a result, the demand for coal and the number of mines increased rapidly.

Mine owners needed a ready workforce, and so they built homes near the mines to house workers' families. Coal towns provided owners with a new, cheaper workforce—women and children.

▶ Watt's steam engine increased demand for coal.

The Welfare of Miners

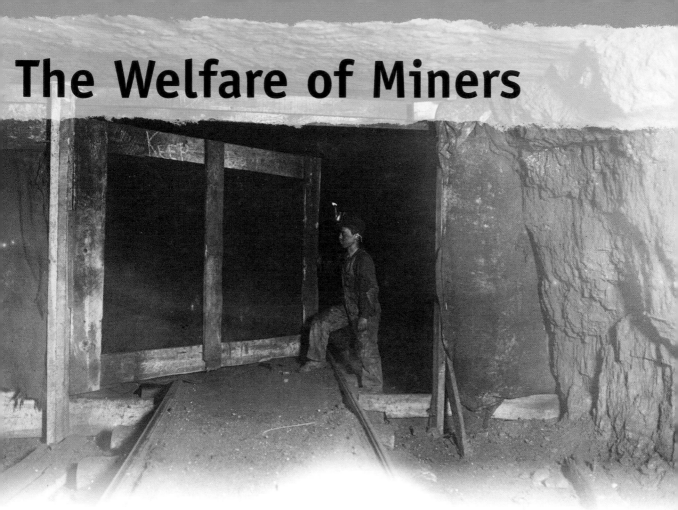

From the 1700s to the mid-1800s, many mining families needed their children to work, to help pay for food and housing. Children started working underground as young as five years old. Although they worked the same hours as their parents, children usually earned half as much money.

▲ Trappers opened wooden doors to let coal and fresh air pass through.

Trappers

Very young children might work as trappers. When tubs of coal moved through mine tunnels, trappers opened and closed the trapdoors. Trappers sat in holes or on low stools for up to 12 hours a day. In 1842 an eight-year-old girl named Sarah Gooder described her work at the Ashley mines in the United Kingdom: "I have to trap without a light and I'm scared. I go at four and sometimes half past three in the morning, and come out at five and half past."

Today, Pakistan, Mongolia, Nepal, Kyrgyzstan, Indonesia, and Colombia still employ children as mine workers. China uses homeless children as coal carriers in mines. The children earn low wages—for example, a boy in a Kyrgyzstan mine earns just $3 a day. But the families of many child mine workers need these wages to survive.

Hurriers

Older children became hurriers. They pulled tubs of coal along narrow passages. Miners used these passages to cut the coal all the way to the pit bottom. Patience Kershaw, a 17-year-old hurrier, recalled: "I hurry the corves [baskets] a mile and more underground and back. They weigh 3 hundredweight [152 kilograms, or 336 pounds]. I hurry 11 corves a-day. I wear a belt and chain at the workings, to get the corves out."

Breaker boys

The use of breaker boys lasted from the 1860s until the 1920s. Breaker boys bent over moving coal, separating **slate** (a thin kind of rock), rocks, and soil from coal. Breaker boys were usually 8 to 12 years old, and they worked 10 hours a day, 6 days a week. After years of work, the boys' backs became permanently bent.

▼ Breaker boys sat for hours picking slate from coal.

Unions bring change

To win better working conditions for all workers, organizations called **unions** were formed. Union members sometimes went on **strike**, meaning they stopped work until demands were met. Throughout history, there have been many coal strikes aimed at improving conditions for workers or saving jobs.

▲ In 1984 the UK government planned to close 20 mines and put 20,000 people out of work. In response, many miners went on strike for a year.

19

Coal and Change

▲ Miners like these provided the coal that fueled industrial growth.

As industries spread worldwide during the 1700s and 1800s, so did the demand for coal. One problem mines faced was getting coal to markets. Building waterways called canals provided a solution, and large ships called barges delivered coal to cities that sprang up along the canals.

A better transportation solution came in 1814, when Britain's George Stephenson introduced a steam locomotive. Trains used coal to generate power, and they hauled coal anywhere tracks were laid. Factories sprang up along railroad lines, and manufacturing expanded.

In the United States during this period, coal mining expanded as iron and steel mills, textile (cloth) mills, and other manufacturing plants blossomed. Coal replaced charcoal as the chief fuel for **iron blast furnaces**. West Virginia joined Pennsylvania as a major coal-producing state.

Social reform

Many people believed that coal mining was too dangerous and unhealthy for women and children. In 1842 the United Kingdom passed the Mines Act, which said that women, girls, and boys under age 10 could not work underground in coal mines. Later, in 1880, school became required for all children in the United Kingdom—which prevented long hours of child labor.

In the United States, West Virginia and Pennsylvania, two major mining states, did not pass laws requiring schooling for children until the late 1890s. Although the Working Men's Party wanted to ban child labor as early as 1876, Arkansas became the first state to forbid child labor in 1914. Later, the Fair Labor Standards Act (1938) included rules about child labor, including setting age limits for children to work.

▼ **Tons of coal moved along U.S. railroad tracks.**

▲ Rescue workers lower water down to three trapped mine workers in 1963.

Safety and health

While profits increased, the health and safety of miners did not. Cave-ins and explosions continued to kill and injure minors. The worst U.S. coal mine disaster took place in Monongah, West Virginia, on December 6, 1907. An underground explosion caused by **methane** gas resulted in the deaths of 362 men and boys.

Throughout the world, many miners have suffered—and continue to suffer—from a disease called black lung, which is caused by breathing coal dust. This quiet killer destroys the lungs. In the United States in 2004, 28 miners died in mine accidents—but 700 died from black lung!

Electricity from coal

The 1900s brought a new power source—electricity—into homes and factories. Lighting switched from open gas lamps to safer electric lamps. Factory machines ran on electric power. Electric trolleys and electric radios also became popular.

As the demand for electric power increased, so did the demand for coal. Burning coal produced the steam to turn turbines and produce electricity.

The rise of petroleum

Coal continued to be the number-one energy source—until the demand for **petroleum** products like gasoline (for cars), heating oil (for homes), and diesel fuel (for trains and trucks) increased. Due to the rise of petroleum, coal production sank to a record low in the early 1950s.

However, shortages in gas and diesel fuel in the 1970s and 1980s brought an increase in coal production. It has increased steadily in recent years, reaching record highs in 2008.

The Upper Big Branch mine disaster ✔

On April 5, 2010, methane gas in the Upper Big Branch mine, in Montcoal, West Virginia, exploded. The explosion caused a cave-in that trapped miners more than 300 meters (1,000 feet) below the surface. Rescuers worked for several days, but 29 out of 31 people trapped inside died.

▼ Cars line up at a gas station in 1978. Shortages in gas and diesel fuel brought about more demand for coal.

23

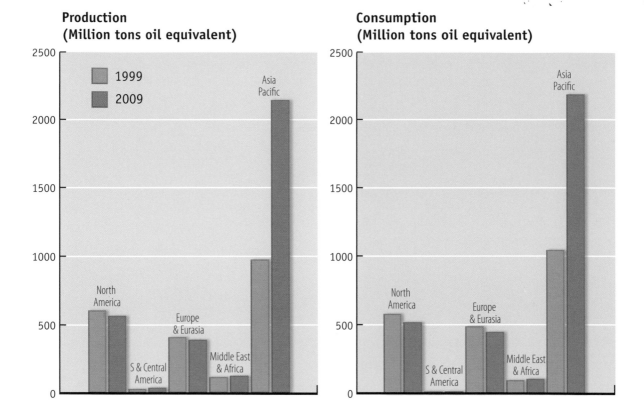

Production
(Million tons oil equivalent)

- 1999
- 2009

North America · S & Central America · Europe & Eurasia · Middle East & Africa · Asia Pacific

Consumption
(Million tons oil equivalent)

North America · S & Central America · Europe & Eurasia · Middle East & Africa · Asia Pacific

▲ Asia and the Pacific, primarily China, produce and consume the most coal.

Coal's worldwide impact

In the 2000s, coal continues to play a major role in generating electricity and powering industry. Several countries produce most of their electricity with coal, including Poland (96 percent), South Africa (90 percent), Australia (84 percent), and China (80 percent). About 56 percent of power in the United States is coal-based, while coal only generates 38 percent of electricity in the United Kingdom.

Coal use is expected to increase by 60 percent over the next 25 years. So, mining companies need to mine as much coal as possible. At the same time, mining safety and careful coal use have become increasingly important.

China is the world's largest coal producer, but it has the worst mine safety record. More than 2,000 Chinese miners have died in explosions and floods there in the past several years.

Coal and the Environment

Environmentalists have concerns about coal. Coal is a **fossil fuel**. When burned, fossil fuels release substances that **pollute**, or dirty, the **environment**.

Surface mining strips plant life and topsoil (the surface layer of soil) from the land. As the coal is washed, coal waste is left behind and pollutes the topsoil. Rain and surface water wash through the mines, picking up chemical waste that pollutes any freshwater sources nearby.

Burning coal to produce electricity also pollutes the air. These polluting chemicals mix with water vapor (water in the form of gas), which becomes acid and returns to Earth as acid rain. This kills plant life.

The solution to coal-related pollution is to use "clean" fuel sources, such as wind power or solar (sun) power.

▲ **Surface mining leaves a scar on the land.**

25

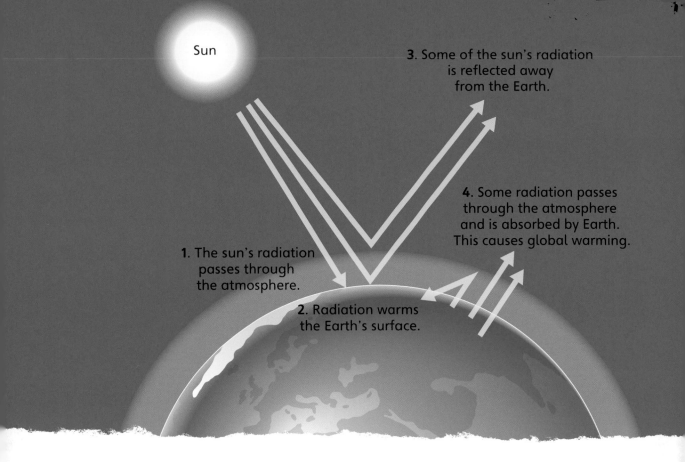

Sun

3. Some of the sun's radiation is reflected away from the Earth.

1. The sun's radiation passes through the atmosphere.

2. Radiation warms the Earth's surface.

4. Some radiation passes through the atmosphere and is absorbed by Earth. This causes global warming.

▲ Greenhouse gases allow more harmful rays of energy to reach Earth's surface.

Coal and global warming

The use of coal and other fossil fuels releases gases like carbon dioxide. These gases, called **greenhouse gases**, build up in our **atmosphere**. They trap extra heat from the sun, acting like the glass in a greenhouse.

We need some greenhouse gases to keep Earth warm enough to live on. But more and more are building up. Earth is experiencing **global warming**, a slow increase in average temperatures. Global warming causes glaciers to melt and seas to rise.

Burning coal adds to this problem, because coal use produces 20 percent of global greenhouse gases. Coal use is increasing in China, India, and Asian countries because it is cheap to use and available. Once these countries build coal-burning power plants, they will be unlikely to stop using coal. This will increase the amount of greenhouse gases in our atmosphere.

Fixing the mess

As we have seen, surface mining greatly damages the land. By law, when mining is finished, mining companies must replace topsoil and plant grasses, trees, and shrubs. This is called land **reclamation**. Reclaimed land becomes animal sanctuaries, parks, farms, and even golf courses.

The technology exists to reduce the effects of coal on our environment. Experts believe we have about 200 years worth of coal remaining. If we replace fossil fuels with "cleaner" energy sources, we may be able to stretch our coal reserves even longer. We need to find solutions to the environmental problems coal presents. If we do, we can continue to use the rock that burns.

▼ Cattle graze on land that was once an open-pit mine.

Timeline

(These dates are often approximations.)

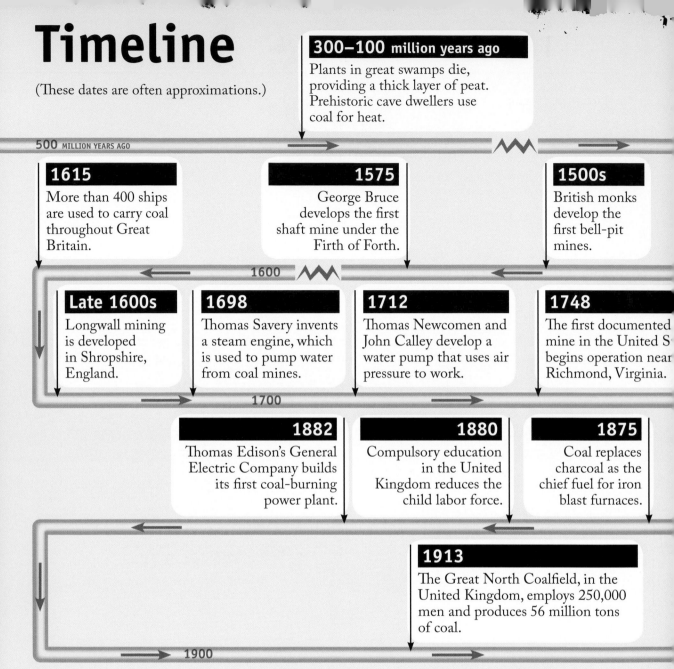

300–100 million years ago
Plants in great swamps die, providing a thick layer of peat. Prehistoric cave dwellers use coal for heat.

500 MILLION YEARS AGO

1615
More than 400 ships are used to carry coal throughout Great Britain.

1575
George Bruce develops the first shaft mine under the Firth of Forth.

1500s
British monks develop the first bell-pit mines.

1600

Late 1600s
Longwall mining is developed in Shropshire, England.

1698
Thomas Savery invents a steam engine, which is used to pump water from coal mines.

1712
Thomas Newcomen and John Calley develop a water pump that uses air pressure to work.

1748
The first documented mine in the United S begins operation near Richmond, Virginia.

1700

1882
Thomas Edison's General Electric Company builds its first coal-burning power plant.

1880
Compulsory education in the United Kingdom reduces the child labor force.

1875
Coal replaces charcoal as the chief fuel for iron blast furnaces.

1913
The Great North Coalfield, in the United Kingdom, employs 250,000 men and produces 56 million tons of coal.

1900

2000

2005
The United States sponsors the construction of the world's first coal-based, "clean" electricity and hydrogen power plant.

28   This symbol shows where there is a change of scale in the timeline or where a long period of time with no noted events has been left out.

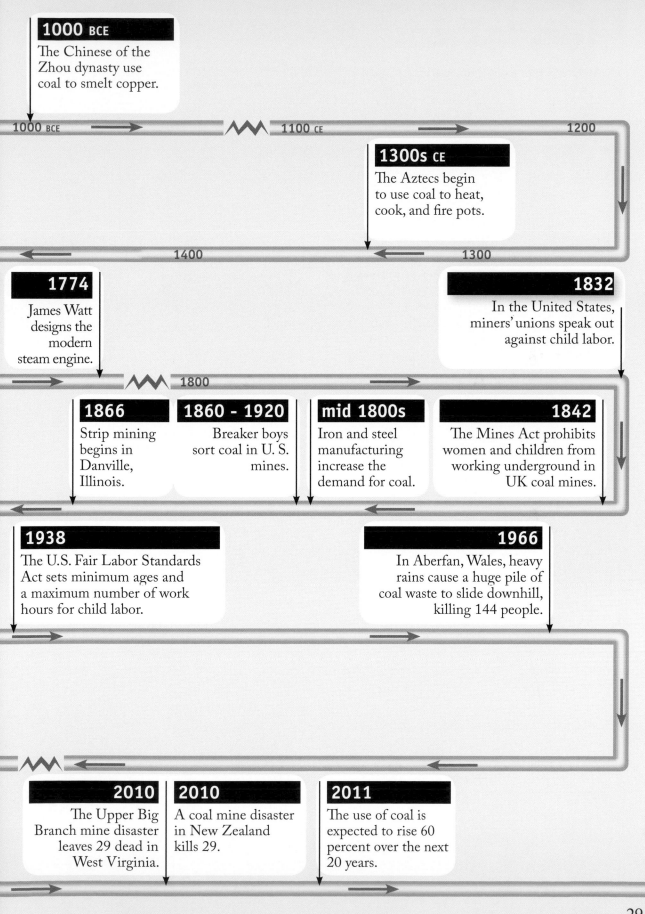

1000 BCE
The Chinese of the Zhou dynasty use coal to smelt copper.

1000 BCE   1100 CE   1200

1300s CE
The Aztecs begin to use coal to heat, cook, and fire pots.

1400   1300

1774
James Watt designs the modern steam engine.

1832
In the United States, miners' unions speak out against child labor.

1800

1866
Strip mining begins in Danville, Illinois.

1860 - 1920
Breaker boys sort coal in U. S. mines.

mid 1800s
Iron and steel manufacturing increase the demand for coal.

1842
The Mines Act prohibits women and children from working underground in UK coal mines.

1938
The U.S. Fair Labor Standards Act sets minimum ages and a maximum number of work hours for child labor.

1966
In Aberfan, Wales, heavy rains cause a huge pile of coal waste to slide downhill, killing 144 people.

2010
The Upper Big Branch mine disaster leaves 29 dead in West Virginia.

2010
A coal mine disaster in New Zealand kills 29.

2011
The use of coal is expected to rise 60 percent over the next 20 years.

Glossary

anthracite hard coal formed under great heat and pressure

atmosphere gas around a planet or moon

bell pit early type of bell-shaped, underground mine

bituminous medium-hard type of coal

coke solid waste product from burning coal

deposit natural collection of minerals or soil

element chemical substance that cannot be divided into any smaller substance

environment air, water, minerals, and living things in an area

fertilizer substance used to help plants grow

fly ash fine particles of burned coal

fossil fuel fuel produced from decayed prehistoric animals or plants

fuel supply with power. The word is also used to mean the substance that helps provide a machine with power.

generate create or produce something

global warming theory that Earth's climate is getting warmer

greenhouse gas gas that absorbs rays from the sun

insecticide substance used to kill insects

iron blast furnace hot oven for melting minerals

lignite soft, brown coal

longwall method of removing coal along a single, long wall of coal

metamorphic rock formed under great heat and pressure

methane odorless, colorless, flammable gas found in coal mines

mill factory for processing raw material

mine place for taking minerals from Earth

mining act or process of taking a substance like coal from Earth

peat layer of plant matter found in marshes or swamps

petroleum crude oil found in rock

pig iron iron cast into large chunks (called pigs) before being used to make steel or cast iron

pollute make the air, water, or soil unclean, usually with waste materials

pressure exertion of great force against an object

reclamation act of restoring to a natural state

room-and-pillar method of removing coal in a grid-like pattern

shaft passage for moving up and down through a mine

slate type of rock

smelt fuse or melt metal

strike refuse to work, usually as a group

subbituminous medium-hard coal with low carbon content

tropical hot, humid climate

turbine machine with a rotor that turns under pressure and produces energy

union organization of workers

winch crank or handle used for lifting or hauling

Find Out More

Books

Green, Robert. *Coal (Power Up!)*. Ann Arbor, Mich.: Cherry Lake, 2010.

Malam, John. *You Wouldn't Want to Be a 19th Century Coal Miner in England!: A Dangerous Job You'd Rather Not Have*. New York: Franklin Watts, 2007.

Skog, Jason. *The Monongah Mining Disaster (We the People)*. Minneapolis: Compass Point, 2008.

Websites

EIA Energy Kids: Coal
www.eia.doe.gov/kids/energy.cfm?page=coal_home-basics
Visit this website sponsored by the U.S. Energy Information Administration to learn more about coal.

National Energy Education Development Project
www.need.org/needpdf/infobook_activities/SecInfo/CoalS.pdf
Learn more about coal at this site designed to answer the question: "What is coal?"

Place to visit

Pioneer Tunnel, Coal Mine, and Steam Train
2001 Walnut Street
Ashland, Pennsylvania 17921
(570) 875-3850
www.pioneertunnel.com
This tourist attraction allows you to see how a real anthracite coal mine works.

Index